_For Mary,
my first &
forever love,
Kath_

Pathways
New and Selected Poems

Kathleen E. Fearing

by

Kathleen E. Fearing

Shamrock Productions
P.O. Box 1206
Norris, TN 37828

Pathways
New And
Selected Poems

For My Sisters

"*We are not what has happened to us, but what we choose to become.*"

Anonymous

Table of Contents

Table of Contents (contd.)

"Poetry is the lifeblood of rebellion, revolution, and the raising of consciousness."

Alice Walker

Pathways

Soft ribbons of sunlight
linger
like hushed thoughts
caught
within the river's morning mist
creating pathways
      to follow
            if I wish

to another way of being
and if the silent night bird
happens to whoosh by
do its feathery tips capture
      a bit of newborn light
           to find its way home…

and Oh! if I spread my own wings

if I follow that silent night bird
thru the deep mystery
of daybreak to wherever it flies
      will I find my own
           pathway

one gentle
filled with light
      unburdened
           as the snowy owl flies…

Dust

Silky clouds of
dry summer dust
drift around my feet
as I walk
settle between my toes
cover my tattered
foot-worn sandals
with a soft persistence
that I
       when returning to my low stool
brush away
thinking it such a pest

but
is it not
the good earth
       that fine dust between my toes

that connects me to
           all that is life…

Fragile Unknown

Some mystery inside me
      quiet
            unspoken

has led me here
      to this forest
            this cool mist

speaks to
      my fragile unknown
            and lately

the need has been great
      to seek
            to find

      to know
            that unknown

Reaching

My hand reaches
through the gentle rush of
late-summer's cool river
to hold
a small
glistening pebble…
      curious
           patient pebble…

somehow knowing
      it rested here
           in the whissshhh
           of wild water

waiting
to tell its untold story
of how
throughout bitter storms

it held strong
      though chunks of it were
      chipped away
      shaping – reshaping its purpose

         yet, it never gave in
         never lost sight of its
         pebble-ness

and as my fingers explore
the pebble's rough scars

I think of my own
telling scars
some visible
others not so much
        hidden in a memory

then
as a mother might to her injured child
the eternal river

        like the serene ageless turtle
        in no great hurry

brushes against
my warm skin
soothing

        my own storm…

Human

The skin feels
the heart loves
the eyes tear
a hand shakes another
arms reach out
to embrace
the hurt child who cries…

how
then
are we different

how?

East Of Here

East of here
east of me
and all that I live now
lies an island
of rambling rock walls
of fields of green
overhung by somber
silver gray clouds
of screeching gulls and roaring
wind-wild surf
of poets and peat
of violence and love
of solitary farms and black-faced sheep
of whiskey and tiny   but
irrepressible shamrock…

an Island of aching beauty
that gave birth to my mother's mother
                and   in quiet memory
                like a home lost to time
        calls to me
                        still…

Chemotherapy

I listened as you spoke
softly, in your calm big sister voice
trying to reassure me
about your chemotherapy
how you were fine
everything was fine
though   your hair
your wild Irish hair
had fallen out
(the curls I was so jealous of
          when we were giddy girls and
          things like hair mattered so
          much)
but you were fine   still
hoping you would keep
your eyebrows at least
and just then I imagined us
together playing laughing
in the grassy yard around
our grandmother's house
when we were ignorant
happy children
hair flying in the wind
wandering the grassy spaces
where summer spews
ecstatic wild flowers
in such profusion
to the young
who see only life
and I wondered

if
in the night
when I was not there
when only quiet
and you
were together
     you cried

Skin

I draw my knees to my chest
smell my naked skin
that human animal skin
that transient shell
that holds all that I am
blood & muscle
warm   alive
and the smell fetches
my head from the fog of uncertainty
back into life…

I am here

      I am alive

         I Am

Places

Places my feet
have wandered
drift back
like an incoming tide
nudging me softly…
a warm hand that gently
turns my head
to face the wind
catching the wild smell of
somewhere far from here
causing a restless ache
that won't leave me
no matter where
I am
how far from there
I wander
or what silence stills me…

…and in one moment
when my heart is soft

I am
        nowhere in particular

yet
        everywhere

One Summer

As one summer
follows the last
and this one now fades
we stand
on the brink of a long dark fall
one where anger
fills the void
where humanity once lived
but the truth has been lost
in a whirlwind of hate
that now howls down every
twist in the road
churning up a choking, blinding
screen…

Michael Legrand
in his longing for
innocence lost
when watching the approach of
war's dark horizon
cried -
  "one last caress,
  it's time to dress
  for fall"

(quote from the theme song to the
movie
"Summer of '42")

Seeking

The heart seeks
what it must
running its course alone
without light or map
to guide its restless way…

Some may
tug at your sleeve saying
go this way   follow me
unaware of how
the sharp lick of flame
burns inside you…

But
there it is
and only you
can feel
the dull ache of
longing   and
where your heart
must go…

For
there is a way
inside you
hidden
perhaps
by anxious ambition
by ego
steering you into the fog…

But
deeper
behind the haze of

      'I must be'

there is a path called

      'I Am'

one suppressed by
wild worldly din

Think
        'my way is there'
           see it
               be it…

Poetry is an echo, asking a shadow to dance."

Carl Sandburg

What Sorrows Me

What sorrows me
women
mirrors of my soul
is even though we
in this unsure world
are one
we are born
bear children
in pain
then release them
into
an unforgiving world
live and work
reach out our arms
toward each other
in heartbreak
in love
in joy
hear the music of life
in the air we breathe
taste bitter tears
ache and grieve
still
we turn to
shout an ugly word
ignore
our shared hurt
why
do we do this
when

after all
our souls
are irretrievably
entwined
let us hear
our fervent calls
and
not
turn
away

Rain

What miracle
is rain
its sweet
fat drops
offer life
without favor
to all
that breathe
and grow
then
in the wake
of a storm's
bitter rage
tear it away
only
to seek out
the hidden seed
and
with the sun
in spring
seduce life back
once
again

The Oldest

First born
she stands
mighty and forbidding
hands on hips
leading the way
we do not
question
but follow
and
love her

Morning Coffee

The smell of coffee drifts
throughout the house
lingering in corners
clinging to walls
it is morning
and though the sun hides from me
it is all good

Rise

Rise
Rise up
      to your
      highest place

Don't wallow in
      the quick of thick mud
      that easy place
      where pity dwells
      and dulls your eyes

Rise
Rise up
      face the cleansing sun

Let it be
      your perfect mother

Names

I carry them with me
a familiar blanket
of ancestral threads
enfolding who I am

they survive
      in the blood
      inherent in my veins

through my hand
      as I struggle
      to write

the bold Irish names
entrusted to me
kathleen and ellen
first and second

      they will never
      pass away

as I am here
so will they be
and may be
long after I disappear

mother and grandmother will live

      I thought forever
      when I was a child

when all things lived loud
when nothing died

now
bits of my tattered blanket fall away
as tired leaves of summer
succumb to a sharp chill

(everything has its time,
I suppose)

now
my finger traces
fading faces
on photos creased in dull memory

(if I close my eyes
I am there   still
small and unquestioning)

now
I strain to recall
fading voices
inside my head

the chaos of crowded Sunday dinners
Mother's sharp Irish tongue

(Kathleen, help your sister set
the table)

the everyday tensions my

mother and grandmothers
long endured

yet
in the naked night
when they whisper to me
when the knots of a web-entangled
world are loosened
when I am alone
comes laughter in a far off thought
a soft brogue
echoing an ancient, green, mossy land –

       these things
       call out their names to me

and I wonder
       is my heart strong enough
       to carry them still

Summer Wanes

(From *When My Feet Were Small, 2016*)

Summer wanes
now the trees grow restless
shedding their summer dress
and crickets hum a
softer hum
estranged apart
few cicadas cling tenuously
to the branches now
birds sense the drift
spending more
and more time on the ground
as if quenching a great thirst
heads bent to grasp
what bugs remain from summer's plenty
and bees hover around
the dying bits of flowers
frantic to capture the last bits of honey
before winter descends
and cold becomes their only thought
though yesterday they owned the air
and all was theirs for the taking…
     Do they ever stop to wonder
          as I do
          grasping my cold feet
          huddling like a lost child
    why summer abandons
    neither looking back
    nor caring what she leaves
    in her shadow?

26

Alive

(From *When My Feet Were Small, 2016*)

The trees come alive
and chat quietly
amongst themselves
like old friends
at the urging of
the wind's gentle hand
and what they speak of
is a secret known only
to them
and tho' I wish it were so
I will never know
      nor did I ever
             even   when   I   knew
      everything
what their whispers
tell   still
I listen hoping
someday
           I might understand.

Nothing Stays

(for Seamus Heaney,
1939-2013)
(From *Now and Then*, 2014)

A blast of wintry air from somewhere
north of here
hugs the valley floor,
leaving its mark,
a killing frost that sears
the leaves of a once
sturdy oak, now
stooped and teetering
at the edge of a river,
unaware it will,
ultimately,
drown,
for nothing stays…
            …but perhaps
a memory,
a voice that echoes
inside your head,
one you heard on a stage,
low and forceful,
singing, the way a poet's
heart sings with life
and knowledge;
seeing what you and I
cannot   but need to;
hearing the unheard;
bowing to what is.

Our Grandmother's House

(From *Women, Poems By Heart, 2011*)

A sister's hard work
keeps it alive.
We sit,
three of us
in yesterday's kitchen,
memories invade our talk,
skip in and out of corners,
October skies hover,
ancient pines spread
around time-hardened timbers.
If we listen,
she is there
with us,
in the walls,
in the attic,
in us.

Letting It Out

(From, *Women, Poems By Heart, 2011)*

I felt my mother in the keyboard strokes
telling me
it's okay,
go ahead,
tell the story…
the story of us.

I heard the forgotten child inside
urging me,
go on,
open the wound,
let it out,
it's all right.

And I told the story.
And I let it out.
And I did not die,
but let yesterday seep away,
so I may live today.

The Audacity Of Weeds
(From *Life Flow, 2015*)

Behold the audacity of weeds,
the way their seedy hair blows in the
wind, sticking out
from the corner
of my garden shed,
hiding at the feet of my roses,
or anywhere they choose
without asking permission,
laughing into the summer air,
and if they had feet, I'm sure
they would run and play as children,
not needing approval,
turning their heads to the sun and,
even tho' pulled up by angry gardeners
they come back again,
and again,
and I want to be like the weeds
not caring,
      just being
wherever I want to be,
unafraid,
      just being.

"Let's admit it. We women are building a motherland; each with her own plot of soil eked from a night of dreams, a day of work. It is a world worth making, a world worth living in, a world in which there is a prevailing and decent wild sanity."

                                    Clarissa Pinkola Estes

May

(From *Life Flow, 2015*)

May,
don't leave me yet,
lay your new sun on my cheeks
until they burn,
wrap your honeysuckle breezes
around my faults and
fill my senses, one,
maybe two afternoons more,
let your newborn leaves sail
on a kind wind, and
if you will, drift soft
through the kitchen window
framed by my mother's faded curtains,
then, over the vines
climbing supple willows to find the sky,
one
maybe two afternoons more.
May,
don't leave me yet,
for I have not had time enough
to hold you in my hands,
not time enough
to know you.

Perfection
(From *Caught In The Crossfire, 2013*)

The child comes
fresh and perfect
a pearl from the oyster
and we revel in her perfection
saying, look, how beautiful,
how sweet,   then
she grows to become
one of us,
hardened, perhaps,
by the business of life,
forced to take a stand
here or there,
we trudge through
the thick mud of life
holding on, remembering
in our darkest moments
the once and fleeting time
of fresh and perfect…
like the foul-smelling flats of the harbor
left bare by ebbing waves,
we long for high tide
to cover and soothe again our
muddy souls.

I Wish

(From *Women, Poems By Heart, 2011*)

I wish
we had known each other
then
before
when you were young
free
happy.

I wish
I could have seen you
smile
laugh
whisper teenage secrets to me
live
be.

I wish
I had known you
then
before
when you were not
my
mother.

Wildflower

(from *Cracklin' Wind, Celtic Dreaming*, 2016)

The wild,
delicate flower
opens its petals to me
slowly, deliberately,
without excitement,
in no particular hurry
or concern
it reveals its inner beauty,
its heart,
its flawless eternity,
and I want to tell
this child of the earth
how it moves my soul to madness,
but all the words I've ever known

                    have left me.

This Wind

(from *Cracklin' Wind, Celtic Dreaming,* 2016)

Take me with you
when you go,
wherever,
whenever…
let me fly with you
in whatever time
or place,
it doesn't matter…
and tell all the others
this wind cannot be divided,
it is what it is.

His Face

His face
       a memory stirs slowly
       like yesterday's stew
       left on the stove
it was good once
when it burst
with life and color
when laughter sparked
like fireflies
round the corners of his mouth
but age dimmed its muscle
       so
       in pain
            its last calling on earth
his face comes back to me
worn by time
spent in the sun
creased by
alcohol and tobacco
a map of despair
held in his eyes
dirt from the field
       where he tended his garden
embedded in the cracks and folds
between his brows
around his blue eyes
still smiling
       despite the web
       of darkness that
       circled him

like a hungry buzzard
until death showed
its mercy.

An Air

There was
then
    (was it really so long ago?)
an air
something to be felt
tasted and lived
    an open door of light
    through which I might
    float   untethered
on a lost summer's day
an air of feathery thought
a lightness of spirit
that lifted me
    upward
in those early days of
my long and rambling life
    upward to the tip top of
    the vibrant oak
a place I felt freedom lived
and a place
    perhaps
        when darkness comes
        and earth closes its eyes

I imagine me
    to be

        still

Where It Can

The tiny bird
makes its nest
where it can

where it can
hidden beneath
an uncertain world

an uncertain world
still it sings
out in the open

out in the open
for its enemies
to hear

to hear
its decree
I Am

I Am

I Am

Wave

I am
a fleeting wave upon the shore
a momentary ripple
on the ocean
of time
where
my heart longs
to leave a sign
across the wide
sandy landscape
a freehand scrawl
only to be
washed away
by a new day's high tide
I am
a fleeting wave upon the shore
but see

I am

Now

Words

Your words came to me
as light through muslin
soft and slightly
just slightly
muted
disguised
but I knew
I knew what you meant
and we both smiled

Sun

Beautiful, soothing sun
light through my morning window
caressing
warming away the chill of fog
cover me with your proud heat
and perhaps
if you linger
the bonds of hate
strangling this tired world
will be diminished
by the peace you spread
with just one glance

You'd Think

You'd think
the bubble of spring
must surely *burst* forth
eager to dance
as soon as sunshine
warms a sleepy April morning…

But…
it makes me   wait
and   wait
doing things
according to
its own
'leave me be' schedule…

And so
I must find
ways to love
                    now

Beyond The Noise

Beyond the noise
the clamor of life
beyond the burning
bottomless pit of blind ego
and lust for power
      (power to silence
      those of a lesser voice)
beyond the noise
there is truth
if we would just

        LISTEN

Owl Mantra

Beautiful one
fly beside me today
help me to see
though it is desperately dark
help me to know
though I stumble
confused
help me listen
to hear
through the chaos
of life
help me be calm
and if I am lost
find me once again

In Praise of Meditation

There are those who, for one reason or another, cannot bear to be still, to listen instead of rant, to sit silently. To those I say, let your mind be still. Relish a quiet moment. Meditate. Listen to the quirks of nature around you: the squirrels rustling through the autumn leaves, the cricket singing its last song in search of love among the low grass and pungent earth. Feel your breath; listen to your heartbeat telling you that you are alive. A young child lying in soft, freshly cut grass watching summer afternoon clouds roll by can do these things, and see how happy she is. Meditate on what is life. Let your mind hear the exquisite, haunting passion of Bach. Be still. Let life itself come to you without expectation. See how rich and beautiful it is when you are still and listen.

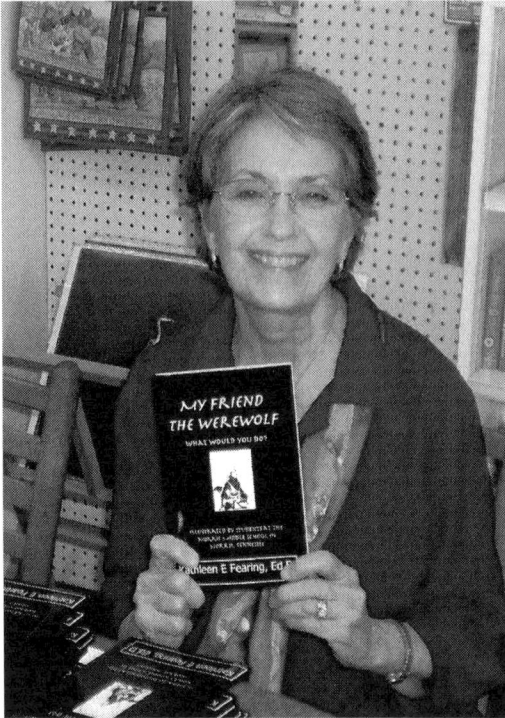

Kathleen E. Fearing has been writing stories for children and poetry for adults for many years. Kathleen has taught children's literature at the college level, is a member of the Appalachian Arts Craft Center, the Tennessee Mountain Writers, the Tennessee Reading Association, and lives with her husband at the foot of the Great Smoky Mountains in Tennessee.

Books by Kathleen E. Fearing
All available at www.Amazon.com

Champ, A Race to Find The Truth,
  2010, 2014
Adisa's Basket, 2010
An Old Heart, Yesterday and Today,
  2010
*My Friend the Werewolf, What Would
  You Do?*, 2011
Women, Poems by Heart, 2011
*Mornings by the River, Poems in the
  Order of Things*, 2011
Voyage of Dreams, An Irish Memory,
  Celtic Cat Publishing,
  Knoxville, TN, 2012
*Caught in the Crossfire, Poems of
  Children in War*, 2013
My Story Time, 2013
Finding Hope, A Reason For Tomorrow,
  2014
Now and Then, Poems & Other Things
  2014
*The Night The Winds Came and Mama
  Sang Her Magic Song*, 2014
Life Flow, 2015
When My Feet Were Small, 2016
A Cracklin' Wind, Celtic Dreaming,
  2016
Voyage Home, 2017

Made in the USA
Columbia, SC
02 August 2019